Elena Iam

<u>Yes!</u>
<u>Science and Religion</u>
<u>Can Coexist!</u>

Is Your God higher than Truth?

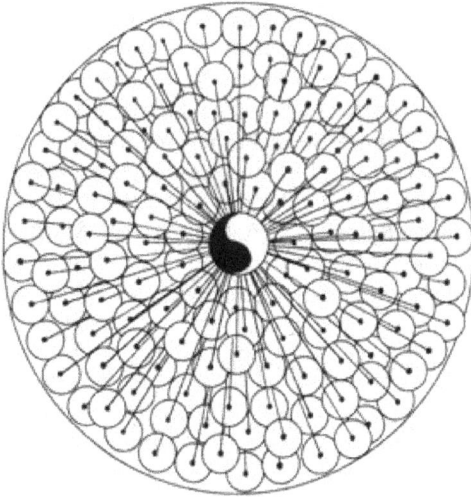

Book Two, System Outlook Series

System Outlook Press, California

Yes! Science and Religion Can Coexist!
Is Your God higher than Truth?
Book Two, System Outlook series

For more information please visit:
www.ScienceAndReligionCoexist.com
www.SystemOutlook.com

Published in the United States of America by System Outlook Press

Please contact Elena for speaking and other business
purposes through her websites:
www.ScienceAndReligionCoexist.com
www.SystemOutlook.com

Library of Congress Control Number: 2014918359

International Standard Book Numbers (ISBN)
Soft cover   978-0-9847090-5-2 (87 pages, 5.5x8.5)
eBook   978-0-9847090-6-9

Special thanks to everyone who helped me with editing and designing of this book: Krista, David, Ellie, Alex and the artist Emma Wright whose artwork is on the cover.

First Edition

Hey there!

It's Elena, the author of System Outlook, a new system-information theory of everything, which unites science and religion and serves as a platform of religious reconciliation.

Have you ever wondered why there are so many religions if there is only one God, or why science and religion are constantly engaged in conflict about the fundamentals of life, and where truth lies? If so, you may find some great insights between the covers of this book. When we look at old arguments from a new perspective, we can suddenly see that debaters usually disregard a number of crucial things. This is the reason why discussions on science and religion go in circles and make no progress.

Questions about God and truth have been my ultimate passion since I was a child. In my quest to seek out the essence of truth I integrated my education on information systems with my deep interest to psychology, philosophy, religion, and spirituality. Thirty years later my journey has culminated in a stunning, unified concept that has embraced all existing information into a complete non-contradictory totality.

The System Outlook approach is based on the axiom that everything in this universe is either a system or a part of a system. It enables us via ultimate all-inclusive principles, which underlie everything in our reality from the smallest particles to massive galaxies. Now it's time to share this knowledge, which gives a truly new impulse for reconciling opposing views and understanding the mystery of God.

This book "Yes! Science and Religion Can Coexist!" is the second in the System Outlook series. I wrote it for a wide audience, mostly young adults, whose minds are open to question everything. This easy-to-read book is not lengthy by volume, but rich with great ideas about beliefs, atheism, fanaticism, public opinions, and minds' illusions.

If you find these ideas interesting and wish to invite me to your group, facility or university for a discussion or debates, please email me at Elena@SystemOutlook.com. I would love to talk to your audience! If you simply feel like sharing your thoughts, please connect to me through the System Outlook page at www.Facebook.com/SystemOutlook.

As my appreciation for your time and interest for this book, I'd like to offer you a **FREE AUDIO GIFT**. Simply go to my website www.ScienceAndRreligionCoexist.com and download there my first one hour CD with excerpts from this book. The name of the CD is "The Big Questions Finally Answered! Introduction to System Outlook."

Also, I would be happy to let you know when we have new publications and free downloads available at Amazon.com.

Table of Content

> *"Only I know what is possible."*
> **God**

> *"Beside all ideas you already have, please notice: you live in a system world, where everything is either a system or a part of a system."*
> **God**

> *"Have you ever noticed that you are born with a natural longing for truth? Look at small children: They are the perfect example of it. They question everything. The day you believe that you are right, you don't care about finding Truth anymore. You turn away from Me."*
> **God**

> *Neither you nor your religion can own the Truth, or gravity, or other laws. All you have is millions of opinions about them."*
> **God**

> **"As God I am Absolute. I embrace all systems including your religions, sciences and beliefs. Not vice versa. None of them can embrace Me."**
> **God**

> **"You live in an illusionary world of your own memory, impressions, and opinions. When you can separate them from the objective laws, you will know the Truth."**
> **God**

> **"I created people, people created fanatics."**
> **God**

> **"Do you know authorities higher than Me?"**
> **God**

> **"How could I be a perfectly good Father if I give all My wisdom to only one child? Why would I leave the rest of My kids with nothing?"**
> **God**

10.

"Sacred scriptures are not about historical events. They contain messages of eternal wisdom, which is one for all. When you look for wisdom, there is no need to argue."
God

11.

"What Gods do you argue about? I don't know them."
God

12.

"If I am not the Truth, then either Me or the Truth don't exist."
God

13.

"You interpret this world through observations either objective reality or subjective experiences. You may call those interpretations scientific discoveries or divine insights. They all describe Me."
God

14.

"I'm not your religion. When you leave your denomination, don't reject Me."
God

> *"I wish I could give people love, money, health and whatever they are praying for right that moment, but… I'm not a vending machine."*
>
> *God*

> *"There is no such thing as the lack of logic. There is a lack of personal understanding."*
>
> *God*

> *"If you want to <u>understand</u> Me, be honest and logical in your search for Truth. If you want to <u>know</u> Me – just talk to Me personally from your deepest sincerity."*
>
> *God*

> *"Your ability to give up your rightness and surrender to Truth, is the gate you allow Me in."*
>
> *God*

> *"When you feel My presence, just simply witness that you personally know Me. Do not assume that your religion is My only dwelling. There is no bottle that can house an elephant."*
>
> *God*

20.

> *"You are more than your mind. You are more than what you think. Observe how computer of your mind creates your opinions and your self-identity."*
>
> *God*

21.

> *"Always practice honesty. It is a shortcut to amazing insights and discoveries."*
>
> *God*

> *"In dual reality, every question has an answer. Some answers simply need time before they are revealed and embraced by human mind."*
>
> *God*

To the memory of the
Three Great Men whose life was
the service to the Truth:
Eminent political leader
__Mahatma Gandhi__,
Metropolitan bishop of
Russian Orthodox Church
__Anthony of Sourozh__,
and __John Templeton__,
One of the greatest business
minds and philanthropists

Foreword

It doesn't matter who we are, what we do, in which country, religion, or era we are born, the search for truth and wisdom is universal. It begins with inner honesty and the deep urge to comprehend the biggest questions in life: what we are, what we live for, why life seems unfair, and so on...

On our journey to understanding truth, we can be taken in different directions. Some find peace of mind within a specific religion, spiritual teaching, or non-denominational eternal wisdom.

The most challenging obstacle on the way to truth is remembering that the truth is, and always will be, more than what we know of it: more than our knowledge, opinions, and any kind of personal experiences. When we are able to separate our personal beliefs and interpretations from objective truth, we then train our minds to *question* every bit of new information instead of shielding ourselves from it and fighting for rightness.

Honesty, humility, and openness are qualities that reflect wisdom and true integrity. When you are grounded in your devotion to truth, you will find the freedom to be yourself and follow your own path.

Often those who belong to the highest political, religious, or business circles face heavy criticism and are blamed for their corruption. We have all heard that "big politics" or "big money" are dirty things.

In reality, there is nothing dirty except for the human intention to dominate others through politics, religion, business, or daily relationships. However, when intention is pure and focused on Truth, its manifestation in this world is incredibly beautiful and outstanding in its positive power.

How many millions of lives were saved due to the wisdom of Mahatma Gandhi, who prevented a war between India and Great Britain? How many people and scientific studies were supported due to John Templeton's philanthropy? How many thousands of souls were impacted by the wise guidance of Anthony of Sourozh?

These three outstanding human beings impacted our lives and world tremendously because they were dedicated to Truth. I hope that we embrace their truthful, humble, and open-minded spirit on our way to understanding Truth while questioning if science and religion can really coexist.

1.
Impossible?... Who said so?...

"Only I know what is possible."
God

Who said it's impossible to unite science and religion? Who said it's impossible to understand God? Who said it was impossible to walk on the Moon?

It was previously impossible, but not anymore. We live in the astonishing age of informational freedom, as well as technological and scientific miracles.

Our current lifestyle was completely unimaginable for our ancestors, even those who lived as recently as one hundred years ago.

When people look toward the future from their present perspective, a lot of their dreams seem impossible because they don't yet have the knowledge necessary for those dreams to become a physical reality.

And it is here that a big problem arises. When our mind cannot find answers or solutions inside of our memory, it gives us an honest response: "There is no solution for now." The sad part: our automatic thinking carries this "negative response" into the future. Our mind creates the false generalization that it should always be so; thus, it makes us to believe that a solution will never be possible for either us or others. This is how a belief takes form and then limits and controls our thinking in the future.

Soon such beliefs become negative axioms, which then block generations of people from even attempting to question that initial negative statement: "Is there really no solution possible? Why not?"

We habitually believe whatever we have been taught. We fail to realize that our negative beliefs shield our mind from genius insights and keep us from searching for new ways of understanding Truth.

When people really want to move forward from endless and fruitless arguments about eternal issues regarding God, truth, and conflict between science and religion, they have to first get rid of the "it's impossible" mindset and the "I'm right" attitude, from which easily spring shallow and sometimes even fanatical perceptions.

There have been a lot of beautiful minds who, regardless of whether they belong to science, philosophy, theology or other disciplines, approach the question of the coexistence of science and religion from a position of honest logic and unity. For them, there never been a conflict between science and religion.

The stereotypical conflict between science and religion is a product of mass media that creates so called "public opinion" on everything. It's a fascinating adventure to explore how true existing opinions actually are.

This book is an attempt to approach habitual stereotypes such as the "conflict between science and religion," the "illogical nature of beliefs," and ideas of God and Truth through a new perspective known as System Outlook. It's a new concept that is based on system-information sciences, as well as an axiom that everything in this world is either a system or a part of a system.

2.

Informational Overabundance

"Beside all ideas you already have, please notice: you live in a system world, where everything is either a system or a part of a system."
God

Can Science and Religion coexist? This question is being asked more often now than ever before. But why?

Currently, the majority of western population is well-educated. People live in a highly technological world, packed with information. We might not see it every day, but informational overabundance is not only a blessing but also a huge challenge. It causes fragmented perceptions and a lack of holistically structured lives. Our subconscious mind has to constantly hesitate while dealing with information: what is right and what is wrong, what is better for us and what is not, which information to focus upon, etc.

Our formal education provides us with various bits of knowledge, such as mathematics, history, language arts, etc. We are not taught, however, how to distinguish true information from false, nor how to make right choices that would benefit us. As a result, after finishing school few of us know how to build a truly fulfilling life.

Our education is based on scientific facts, discoveries, and methodology. We learn that our outer world is logical, hierarchical, and systemic. Conversely, we have deep psychological needs that sciences may not address. We need love, acceptance, security, happiness, and freedom from our fears. We need to know that our life makes sense even during times of pain and severe suffering.

Those needs have been traditionally related to the soul and addressed by religious or spiritual teachings. Today, however, we have a problem: thousands of religious denominations offer numerous ideas about God, truth, and the meaning of life. Who is right? The more information we have, the more questions arise. It's an overwhelming situation for those who seek to understand the Truth about our reality and the phenomenon of our existence.

You may have heard this famous joke:

- Dad, what is the truth?
- Sorry, son. I cannot tell you. The Internet is down.

People have been debating about the Truth and the purpose of life for thousands of years. Nevertheless, those biggest questions are still not being answered in a way that is acceptable to everyone. It seems that even the Internet doesn't have a solution though it keeps billions of answers for nearly every question in its virtual informational library.

I discovered these questions very early, around eleven years old, because I was a very sensitive child in a dysfunctional family. My parents were well-educated but not wise at all. My desire to be happy triggered too many questions: Why do people suffer? Why does love end? Why did I get such parents? What's more important: to be wise, wealthy, or educated? And how can I know the Truth?

We usually never ask these questions when everything is fine. We live life on autopilot, without much thinking. We take our comfort for granted and tend to just assume that life is meant to be this way all the time.

As it happens, fate often changes plans, and sometimes strikes us with sudden challenges. It has an entire arsenal of random dramas and tragedies: Terminal disease, depression, death, betrayal by loved ones, etc. Many of us know how painful it is.

We wake up at those moments and yell at the universe, asking why life is so unfair. Where is God and why does He allow such suffering?

These are the times when many people embark on their spiritual journey. They look to understand questions that suddenly became very big. Where is the Truth? And where is God in this life?

Today we are blessed to have a total spiritual freedom. We can freely explore truth through science or any existing religious or spiritual tradition.

However, this situation was very different only a couple centuries ago. People had no spiritual freedom and didn't yet understand democracy. For thousands of years, local religions had a monopoly on truth and addressed all the Big Questions in a certain simple way. Each religion offered its followers a specific system of beliefs, so those people had very clear ideas about God and their life purpose.

Religious systems explained how the world operates. They offered various stories about how the universe was created and how people should behave in order to live in harmony with daily challenges: exhausting work, death, diseases, slavery, wars, evil neighbors or kings… Religions helped people to have a holistic perception and balance adversities with a promise of Heaven, a reward in the afterlife for 'good' behavior.

Very few people questioned their religious beliefs as there was no alternative information. The majority of people were illiterate. They didn't understand science. For instance, my grandparents were born in the beginning of the 20th century in Russia. Even that recently, however, my Grandma never learned how to read and my Grandpa could only read very slowly.

Today the situation is different. People spend at least ten-twelve years in school, plus time in colleges and universities. We have immediate access to unlimited information, thanks to the Internet. Everything we need is just a click away. We can instantly learn about ancient religious beliefs or the latest scientific discoveries, not to mention thousands of theories that belong to philosophy, psychology, spirituality, and other fields.

This astonishing informational overabundance, however, creates not only possibilities but also confusion. We are left to then ask where to find Truth in the midst of so much information and contrary opinions.

3.

<u>*Are you sure that you are right?*</u>

"Have you ever noticed that you are born with a natural longing for truth? Look at small children: They are the perfect example of it. They question everything. The day you believe that you are right, you don't care about finding Truth anymore. You turn away from Me."
God

It is no coincidence that in America, debates related to God, science, and religion have become more popular in the last decade than ever before. We absorb incredible amounts of contradictory information everyday. It can be confusing for our minds when we don't know how to unite all of these pieces of information into one clear non-contradictory picture that reflects the reality of our life.

Until our minds are capable of uniting information into one logical structure, wherein we are able to sort out truthful knowledge from the false, the questions regarding what is right and what is wrong don't arise. Our hesitations begin the moment that we have to logically evaluate contradictory and competing information.

Which medicine would help soothe a stomach ache faster? Which candidate would be a better president? Which religion should we believe in: Christianity, Islam, Buddhism, Paganism?

The fact is that science says nothing about God or religion. It makes the situation even more uncertain. How can we know if God really exists and which idea of God is true? How can we find evidence that would prove that our life has a particular purpose instead of being just a random psycho-physiological phenomenon?

What we are? How would our lives be different if we could know, with complete certainty, that we are not just mere biological organisms that will eventually turn into the dust of this senseless cold universe? Depending on how we explain those questions to ourselves, our mind creates patterns of our reactions and daily behaviors that directly affect all our choices, big and small.

Feelings of happiness, love, and fulfillment - or the lack of them - are the final outcome of our perception and attempts at understanding the truth about what this life is supposed to be.

Most people miss the practicality of the idea of truth. On the surface the ideas of truth and happiness hardly seem related. In daily life, people generally relate their happiness to various kinds of pleasures. They rarely notice that the feeling of stable, lasting fulfillment is generated by their beliefs about life, not by occasional fun, luck, or goodies.

Many people push away thoughts about "the meaning of life" or "truth" as these big questions seem to have no clear answer and feel too "heavy" to contemplate. So these questions end up being left to scholars who enjoy philosophical arguments and theoretical reasoning.

Alas, observation and attentiveness to inner thoughts and motivations are not a part of western culture. This the reason that people rarely recognize the fact that they are born with a strong instinctive need to know the truth about everything, especially things that affect their personal world, including their well-being, relationships, and finances. What is curiosity but a desire to know the truth about something or somebody?

When we know the truth about any aspect of our life, uncertainty diminishes and we feel more secure. We feel more confident as we see how to reach our goals faster and achieve the results we want. Truth brings clarity and dissolves illusions, giving us a clear understanding of our best choices.

Have you ever thought about the ways in which our world has so dramatically changed as a result of science discovering the truth about the physical laws that rule reality in which we live?

Once people gained understanding of natural and mathematical laws, they immediately applied this knowledge towards improving their quality of life with such conveniences as electricity, hot water, automobiles, airplanes, computers, etc.

Imagine how different out world could be if science could successfully discover the truth of the laws that rule over the intangible realm of our thoughts and feelings?

With such knowledge, we would no longer doubt if ethical laws are imperative for everyone or not. Additionally, the knowledge of ultimate Truth would give us a holistic vision of our existence: We would know, with complete certainty, whether our physical lives are senseless or if they are precious links in an endless chain of eternal experiences. But traditional physical and natural sciences have nothing to say about the matter, instead leaving the question of ultimate Truth open to the controversy of religious beliefs, philosophical debates, and the recently developed interdisciplinary field of system-information sciences.

4.

Public Opinion?... Give me a break!

"Neither you nor your religion can own the Truth,
or gravity, or other laws. All you have is
millions of opinions about them."
God

It's no wonder that the more information is available, the more arguments people have.

You may have heard – perhaps many times - that there is no God, because science said so. Or maybe instead you have heard that religion is the only true way and that prophets' ancient words are far truer than anything else, including scientific data and discoveries.

Those statements are classic examples of the argument between atheists and religious fundamentalists. These strong assertions float on the surface of all disagreements and create an impression of an irreconcilable fight between science and religion. Once, during a debate at a California university, a young man passionately stated that science and religion have been in perpetual conflict for thousands of years.

When I asked if anyone else thought the same way, more than half of the students immediately raised their hands. Does this mean that believing in the conflict between science and religion is a common opinion? It's quite possible. When we constantly hear about arguments related to God, Truth, faith, religion, or modern sciences, we inevitably create the impression that there must be a conflict.

However, is there really a conflict or is this just a false impression?

Public opinions are often superficial and have little to do with reality. It's hardly a secret that public opinions are mostly formed by those who control the information broadcast through radios, TVs, and newspapers.

The end result is that the average consumer of information has a cocktail of ideas, historical facts, church sermons, latest political scandals, and controversial quotes from television personalities. When all these fragments of information are blended together, it is barely possible to extract the "truth."

Most people never bother to investigate the truthfulness of statements made by mass media gurus, school teachers, or local preachers. They tend to trust authorities and thus free themselves from the necessity of critical and independent thinking.

We have plenty of examples from educational history, through which millions of people adopted beliefs without much questioning; the result of such weak critical thinking turned into grandiose tragedies like the Soviet Communist Empire and Hitler's Germany.

"The perpetual conflict between science and religion" is one of those unquestionable beliefs formed by deceitful impressions, barely ever analyzed by mass culture or current educational system.

Today, when we face contradictory information, it is extremely important to be careful and observant to the origins of our beliefs and to what we accept as "truth."

When we feel like making a strong statement such as "there is a conflict between science and religion," we should first make an effort to at least check Wikipedia, which has lately become the best online source of unbiased knowledge and information.

Here is a quote taken from Wikipedia in December of 2013 on the coexistence of science and religion:

> While the conflict thesis remains popular for the public, it has lost favor among most contemporary historians of science.
>
> Many theologians, philosophers and scientists in history have found no conflict between their faith and science. Biologist Stephen Jay Gould, other scientists, and

some contemporary theologians hold that religion and science are non-overlapping magisteria, addressing fundamentally separate forms of knowledge and aspects of life.

Scientists Francisco Ayala, Kenneth R. Miller and Francis Collins see no necessary conflict between religion and science. Some theologians or historians of science, including John Lennox, Thomas Berry, Brian Swimme and Ken Wilber propose an interconnection between them.

Isn't it interesting how diametrically opposed this view is to that of the generally accepted public opinion? To many of the best contemporary scholars and scientists, there is no conflict between religion and science.

We tend to avoid questioning the truthfulness of scientific authorities. In this case however, it is important to better understand why there is no such conflict, especially when debates on the coexistence between science and religion become increasingly popular, and more people leave their traditional religions than ever before.

5.
How to untangle... opinions?

_"As God I am Absolute. I embrace all systems
including your religions, sciences and beliefs. Not
vice versa. None of them can embrace Me."_
God

There are innumerable arguments related to religious
or scientific views, and plenty of disagreements between
existing religions and spiritual teachings, atheists and
believers, as well as differences in scientific and religious
methodology of obtaining information, etc. It reminds one
of a big tangled bundle of many brightly colored threads.

Each opinion is like a thread of a certain color and
texture taken from differently colored pieces of cloth,
maybe a warm blue woolen sweater or a white cotton shirt.
It's useless to argue which thread is "better" or "makes
more sense." Opinions, like threads, make more sense
when we can see the entire context or system (cloth, in this
example) to which they belong.

When people enter disputes, they are so obsessed with
the rightness of their view that they seldom notice that they
argue from perspectives of specific systems, which are not
compatible: like Christianity and physics or Buddhism and
cosmology. Furthermore, people confuse God with religion,

and objective laws with science.

To untangle all these threads and finally understand what is what, we have no choice but to approach this problem with systematic methods in order to define and distinguish the systems we are talking about.

For instance, when God and religion are blamed for the crimes committed during the Spanish Inquisition, it is important to understand that this statement is logically incorrect as God and religion are not synonymous; instead they are independent systems. The system called "God" is ultimate, objective, and all-inclusive phenomenon; a system called "religion" is a set of subjective interpretations of God that totals more than hundreds of thousands teachings, beliefs, and organizations.

Who holds responsibility for religious crimes? God as the initial cause of this universe? Systems of religious beliefs about God? Or religions as political systems, which pursue their selfish interests at certain historical moments?

When we define these systems, we can clearly see that crimes committed by the Inquisition are the product and responsibility of a system of the religious politics, **not** the systems of Christian beliefs or God.

That is only one brief example showing how a

systematic approach helps eliminate arguments and hostility by developing a deeper understanding of what we actually are talking about. The same approach can be successfully used with any other complex or painful issue that seems to lack any possibility of reconciliation.

In order to reach the issue at the heart of a complex problem like the coexistence of science and religion, we have to separate this problem into different issues and related systems, then analyze them from unbiased perspectives of the system-informational approach.

6.

Impressions, Opinions, Delusions…

"You live in an illusionary world of your own memory, impressions, and opinions. When you can separate them from the objective laws, you will know the Truth."
God

Let's explore the common impression that there is a longstanding conflict between science and religion. As we already have mentioned, this impression is both illusive and unshared by many contemporary historians, theologians and scientists.

However, if arguments among public about science and religion have become louder than ever before, it is important to look closely at the causes supporting this delusive impression. At the same time we should consider the emotional component, which is a part of perception that often plays the main role in creating our opinions.

The primary cause of this public delusion springs from the fact that we live in a secular society where religion is separated from the state and education system. When the words "God" and "religion" become "taboo" and forbidden in public school, our mind interprets this as a veiled message that "something," in this case, God and religion, is probably illegitimate or untrustworthy.

In reality, the reasons why religion is separated from the educational system may sound quite sensible; subconsciously, however, our mind perceives and registers a subtle feeling that religion maybe unsafe or even sort of "wrong." Additionally, modern educators teach students to respect proven facts, logic, and formulas. This approach is insufficient for understanding ancient spiritual scriptures. As a result, religious texts and parables seem illogical and not legitimate when compared with scientifically based books for many students.

The second aspect, which creates an impression of conflict between science and religion, is historical. When people learn about religious wars, the Inquisition, witch-hunting, and the persecution of the first scientists (who were burned at the stake along with their scientific manuscripts), the immediate reaction is to blame religious fanaticism. The mind often then jumps to the conclusion that religion fought science for centuries. This conclusion is incorrect.

Human history reveals many religions that have never clashed with developing sciences and scientific discoveries. Instead, monasteries and their libraries had been spiritual and educational centers for centuries. They carefully collected knowledge not only from holy scriptures, but also from the first scientific researches, theories, and treatises. Often the first scientists were monks, who were usually the most educated people in their societies.

Yes, there were times when blazing fires all over the Europe burned priceless scientific books, but those fires were not generated by the "conflict" between science and religion. Those fires and hatred toward progress or dissenting opinions were caused by autocratic religious systems, which had to protect their power and ideological influence over the masses.

When "religion" as an organization fights for followers and

money, it behaves no better than a political party or a despotic regime. It destroys everything in the way of its power.

Religions as political systems do not care which ideas they silence if those ideas are not in alignment with current official doctrines. Religions easily attached the label "heretic" to anyone, whether that so-called blasphemer was interested in scientific discovery or held pagan or alternative Christian beliefs.

Religious wars and massacres are historically a part of many cultures and religious traditions. Catholics, Jews, and Muslims have been fighting each other for centuries, as well as against their fellow countrymen who prayed to the same God in a slightly different way. We all know about the bloody massacres perpetuated time and again between two Muslim factions: the Sunni and Shiite. Muslims are not the only culprits; Saint Bartholomew's Night massacre against French Calvinist Protestants in 1572 was directed by French Catholics.

How are these religious wars related to science? They are **not connected** at all! Science has never been anything but a system of independent, objective knowledge. Any knowledge as a system is neutral in nature, regardless of whether it is scientific, religious, or spiritual.

If people use scientific knowledge to create atomic bombs or weapons of mass destruction, the political system that uses these creations to inflict harm on other countries has nothing to do with the science itself, nor those scientists who made amazing discoveries about atoms and other elementary particles of the micro-world. The same rules apply for religions.

Fights, wars, genocide, and hatred have been never initiated by a system of religious beliefs or spiritual knowledge. Instead, religious organizations that had to expand their political power over others are those who are responsible for blood of innocent.   It is important to understand this in order to avoid blaming all Muslims or all Christians who sincerely believe in their prophets and scriptures.

7.

How to clone fanatics

> *"I created people, people created fanatics."*
> *God*

The mechanism of inciting hostility against outsiders and creating armies of fanatics is always the same: it's called brainwashing. The moment a religious or political leader convinces his followers that they are a superior group among humans, they justify the domination, hostility and even destruction of outsiders. In the name of perceived superiority, these fanatics abuse other groups for the sake of their doctrine, whether that be God, the "Aryan race," communism, democracy, or any number of other causes.

Some people believe that fanaticism is a product of religious systems. That is not quite true. I would say that fanaticism is an individual mental quality that can be defined as an obsessive zeal coupled with a lack of critical thinking. Fanatics belong not only to religions. There are also fanatics in politics, sports, extraterrestrial-belief, communism, atheism, and even science. Those who have never questioned their rightness are already half-way to becoming real fanatics. As soon as those people affiliate themselves with a like-minded flock, whose large numbers reaffirm their beliefs and rightness, they move another step toward the classic definition of "fanatic."

Thus, opposing religious fanaticism with science is logically incorrect. Scientific knowledge and the mental state of narrow-mindedness are not mutually exclusive. They simply belong to different domains, like trains and butterflies.

If there is still a need to oppose *religious* fanaticism, then one must also oppose *atheistic* fanaticism, as both are similar mindsets that focus on opposite beliefs.

The next factor that often causes people to see a conflict between science and religion is a recent trend in which people are abandoning their traditional religions. Popular opinion calls this a sign that people are choosing science over religion.

That is not so. The majority of those who quit their denominations do not become scientists, and they do not even necessarily care about the sciences. Whatever reasons bring people to leave their traditional faiths, those reasons cannot be said to be related to science or the opposition between science and religion.

8.

Big names magic: or who is your authority?

"Do you know authorities higher than Me?"
God

When people argue about science and religion, trying to justify their righteousness, they often support their position with famous quotations. Debaters mostly use the names of famous scientists or other well-known thinkers, like Voltaire or even Hemingway, as if their quotes on the subject of "God" could somehow add more weight to their personal position.

Funny enough, words from scientific giants like Newton, Darwin, or Einstein are used equally by both parties of the 'debate:' those who claim the existence of God as well as those who insist that this universe is random and has no place for divine presence.

I do not want to say that some debaters intentionally manipulate information in order to win support from listeners, but when we pay closer attention to their arguments we can see that their claims are sometimes irrelevant or even hilarious.

In one debate I recently watched online, one popular debater made a wide claim that great scientists have never accepted God as a serious idea worthy of their time. As a confirmation of his position, he presented a famous phrase that "all thinking men are atheists," attributed to Ernest Hemingway. While Hemingway was definitely a talented writer, his name cannot be related to the sciences by any means!

Such zeal for rightness often triggers many debaters to shamelessly quote big-name scientists or other authorities out of context. Sadly, twisting famous quotations is not a rare thing. Thus it is important to be able to critically analyze all statements presented as "scientific" truth.

By exploring the religious views of those who we consider the pillars of modern sciences, we will see that their lives were dedicated to understanding the Truth. Their personal religious views might not have been in alignment with the current religious systems or doctrines, which required obeying rigid rules and dogmas, but those marvelous scientific minds were the first to understand the difference between religion as a human-made system and God as initial cause of all creations.

If you have ever being told that great scientists like Isaac Newton, Louis Pasteur or Max Plank opposed the idea of God, please look at the quotes below and consider going online to search for their other quotations. You will be surprised to find that among the greatest authentic scientific minds, you can barely find those who outright rejected the idea of the Creator.

"Gravity explains the motions of the planets, but it cannot explain who set the planets in motion. God governs all things and knows all that is or can be done."

Isaac Newton, 17th century

"That we must love one God only is a thing so evident it doesn't require miracles to prove it."

Blaise Pascal, 17th century

"If you study science deep enough and long enough, it will force you to believe in God."

Lord William Kelvin, 19th century

"Little science takes you away from God but more of it takes you to Him."

Louis Pasteur, 19th century

"So, I feel compelled to look to a First Cause having an intelligent mind; and I deserve to be called a Theist."

Charles Darwin, 19th century

Here are several quotes of modern scientists of the twentieth century:

"The more I study science, the more I believe in God."

Albert Einstein, 20th century

"Both religion and science require a belief in God. For believers, God is in the beginning, and for physicists He is at the end of all considerations... There can never be any real opposition between religion and science; for the one is the complement of the other. And indeed it was not by accident that the greatest thinkers of all ages were deeply religious souls."

Max Planck, 20th century

These are but a handful from hundreds of quotations from scientists about God and science. Many of these scientists have won the Nobel Prize in their fields. They do not have a problem with God and do not see a conflict between science and religion.

9.

From "Who is Right" to "What is true"

"How could I be a perfectly good Father if I give all My wisdom to only one child? Why would I leave the rest of My kids with nothing?"
God

Debates and debating is the fifth (and perhaps most visible) factor suggesting that science and religion endlessly fight. Debates on God and sciences begin in high school. In colleges and universities the conversation becomes more intense due to the students' spirit of daring and freedom. Finally, mass media contributes to these debates with sparkles of "hot news," seeking to agitate and gain attention while adding catchy headlines to articles like "Have scientists really found a particle of God?"

I love to watch debates and Youtube is an amazing source to find hundreds of videos featuring the best thinkers and debaters of our time. For me, debates are sort of an intellectual sport, like boxing or wrestling for the brain. However, it seems that debaters rarely care about the Truth while on stage; in most cases they simply present their position and try to be witty in order to make fun of their opponents and catch the audience's attention. This tactic is definitely entertaining, but it does not help to illuminate a path to the *actual* Truth.

Another reason why debates do not move anywhere is linguistic confusion. Usually, debaters do not bother to distinguish God from religion or science from scientific perception; they do not see any difference between religion as a system of beliefs and religion as a political system, etc.

Finally, here is the most important point why debates in their modern form fail to produce fresh and productive insights on the essence of Truth: ultimate ideas like God, Truth or the meaning of life cannot be contested from the non-ultimate perspectives of isolated systems that have nothing in common. Various sciences and religions are examples of such isolated information systems. Comparing cosmology and Christianity is similar to comparing music and history. We can share our passions for the latest discoveries, ancient scripts, spiritual music, or historical researches, but what's the point if we do not synergize existing knowledge and opinions?

New insights always grow from the synergy of existing knowledge. The abundance of information gives modern people the very unique opportunity to play with existing information by analyzing every bit of it on the way to discovering Truth. However, minds of those who seek only to prove the correctness of their Christian, Muslim, or atheistic doctrines are firmly shut to possible updates on their understanding of Truth.

Let's shift our attention to *what* is true, rather than to *who* is right. Let's look for commonalities behind prophetic words, ancient scripts, and discovered scientific laws. When we reject a system of any knowledge, we overlook the fact that all existing information systems reflect at least some elements of objective universal laws, though from narrow standpoints. Human perception and understanding is limited by the amount of knowledge available at certain moments in history.

For this reason, we cannot compare primitive polytheism with monotheism or quantum physics as these three informational systems originated during different historical periods. When understood from this perspective, primitive polytheism is no less valid than modern science. Thousands of years ago, it was the only available perception of reality and was therefore true for our ancient ancestors.

The challenge is to find a platform that helps unite and reconcile all of existing ideas of Truth into one unified and non-contradictory vision.

10.

Blind men's debates

"Sacred scriptures are not about historical events. They contain messages of eternal wisdom, which is one for all. When you look for wisdom, there is no need to argue."
God

There is an ancient story that originated in India about wise blind men who argued over which of them was right. They explored different parts of an elephant, touching the elephant's trunk, tail, and massive legs. They could not stop arguing with each other about what the elephant actually was: a type of hose or pillar or rope. This story is a famous reflection of religions trapped in their rigid interpretations of God and blind to seeing the whole picture.

Today we could add atheists, agnostics, and scientists to this company of blind wise men and the situation would not change. They all would continue arguing and call it "debate."

Let's recall a typical debate scenario, where each participant repeats his opinion, one based on his personal knowledge and belief system.

In debates, everyone tries to justify their vantage points using logic. Unfortunately, their logic does not extend beyond their own informational system and they are unable to relate to their competitor's logic and information. How could people understand each other if the logic of physics has nothing to do with the logic of religion? Thus, cosmology, Christianity, and microbiology relate to each other no more than a hose, pillar, and rope relate.

As a result, debates on God, science, and religion are deadlocked. They go in circles and are unproductive.

To actually understand the Truth (or to see the "whole elephant"), it's necessary to **want** to go beyond our personal habitual interpretations of reality. It is also important to be honest when we are questing for Truth. Finally, we must have an ultimate system that would allow us to harmoniously unite all existing information into one totality in order to successfully approach questions of coexistence between science and religion as well as the fundamental principles of human life.

Now, in the 21st century, this has become possible due to the development of computer-related system-information sciences. We will deeper dive into this in later chapters, but first let's take a look at the questions most often featured in debates.

11.

Firstly, define what your God is!

"What Gods do you argue about? I don't know them."
God

From my observations, people mostly debate the questions of if there is God, if God is good, and if it makes sense to believe in God. The discussions about **what** God is, or about the essence of God, are not so popular.

Here lies the first problem: when people start arguing about God, without defining what God is, they will never come to any agreement.

Years ago, back in my university days, I studied a very interesting subject called "informational linguistics." One of the basic concepts of informational linguistics was the necessity of having clear definitions to apply to words used in negotiations, contracts, computer programs, or disputes. Without clarifying the functions and definitions of words, which are the linguistic elements in every system, the systems cannot function properly. If one word, like the word "God," has several interpretations, it creates confusion among those who use this word while negotiating or arguing.

Religious fundamentalists may see God as a specific doctrine or entity: Christ, Trinity, Allah, or Yahweh, for example.

Atheists, in turn, fight against any and all religious doctrines. For instance, they point at the unfair struggle in the Biblical story of Job, and call God a cruel maniac whose existence does not make sense.

As to modern spiritual seekers, plenty of them associate God with so-called "conscious energy."

At the same time, many great scientists admire God as the absolute intelligent mind who created our universe.

"This most beautiful system of the sun, planets and comets, could only proceed from the counsel and dominion of an intelligent and powerful Being."

Isaac Newton; *17th century*

"As a man who has devoted his whole life to the most clear headed science, to the study of matter, I can tell you as a result of my research about atoms this much: There is no matter as such. All matter originates and exists only by virtue of a force which brings the particle of an atom to vibration and holds this most minute solar system of the

atom together. We must assume behind this force the existence of a conscious and intelligent mind. This mind is the matrix of all matter."

Max Planck; 20th century

The question then becomes the following: about which God people are arguing? It is clear that Newton's God has nothing in common with certain sacred religious images, regardless of whether those images describe angels, sacred symbols, or anything else.

If religious fundamentalists form their ideas of God from religious scripts and specific dogmatic definitions of God, then the God of "spiritual" scientists has always been the higher Truth that defines human life, either through physical or moral laws.

It seems evident to non-fundamentalists that God cannot be diminished to a narrow interpretation or definition. Such a narrow interpretation could only fit one out of thousands of teachings, therefore excluding all other knowledge accumulated by humankind throughout history.

Humanity as a single system has been growing through different stages of mental and spiritual development. Primitive beliefs turned into polytheism; thousands of years passed and the human mind was ready to absorb an abstract monotheistic idea of a single omnipresent God. From a

Judaic prospective, the essence of God could be summarized with only one word: the "Law." It is no wonder that scientific development had become the next stage in understanding the essence of God, now through objective observations and discovering particular laws that rule systems of our surrounding physical reality.

What is the truth about this universe? Is there something beyond the physical world which our senses make us aware of? What forms this reality? What called this world and each of us into existence? What kind of laws and patterns make our bodies work the same way and feel the same feelings, from the finest joy to the deepest sorrow?

What is the source which generates the laws that form this magnificent reality of our universe as well as the unique realities of our inner worlds? Scientists call this source "the Truth."

Humankind is slowly approaching the mystery of the initial Truth with each new scientific discovery, and also with personal intuitive insights.

It does not matter which area of life we talk about, Truth will always be the final destination. When we know the laws of a system we know the Truth, which liberates us from hesitations and arguments. We gain confidence to act upon the Truth; we move forward and create new, better experiences.

When we know the truth about the laws of gravity, for instance, we get a chance to fly to the Moon. When we know the truth about our relationship, finances, or health, we get an opportunity to make the best choices and avoid pain.

Is it there something in this world that is not the subject of arguments? Absolutely! Formal disciplines, mathematics, physical, and natural laws proven by formulas can fit this measure. Arguments fade away under the power of logical proof.

There is a common expression that it is impossible to prove the existence of God. If knowledge of God is nothing more than the result of a personal experience, then yes, it would never be possible to prove your personal feelings and experiences to anyone who cannot relate to them, or who has never experienced anything like that.

However, to diminish God to the level of only our own mystical experiences and interpretations would make God nothing more than a product of our subjective perception and imagination. If God exists, God has to be far more than all our thoughts, feelings, and ideas all together.

12.

Is God something else but Truth?

*"If I am not the Truth, then either Me
or the Truth don't exist."*
God

Here we hit a crucial point – is there a difference
between God and Truth?

Are God and Truth two different phenomena or just two
different words that define the same single and objective
source of everything?

Mahatma Gandhi once said, "There is no God higher
than Truth." Take a minute and contemplate those genius
words.

Whatever interpretation of God you believe, try to
separate your ideas of God from the real God. This should
be similar to the realization that your personality is far
more than all opinions other people have about you.
Similarly, your parents, the president of your country, or a
certain celebrity are far more than just your thoughts and
feelings about them.

I love brain teasers. They require us to be absolutely
honest with ourselves. Can God be something other than
the absolute Truth? No. God and Truth are the only two
ideas that possess such qualities as singleness,

50

absoluteness, eternity, and omnipresence. There cannot be any situation in which God and the Absolute Truth would exist next to each other. The logic to this is simple:

If God is, then God has to be Truth.

If God can be something else but Truth, then God is not Truth, and consequently God does not exist.

Gandhi's words are absolutely brilliant. They mean that if God is, then He cannot be anything else but Truth. If we take all the names people have given to God through all of history, "Truth" would be the only name that could act as a substitute for every definition of the word "God" while also satisfying everyone.

I was asked once: if God and the Absolute Truth are one, then why is it that, historically, the ideas of God and Truth have often been separate rather than united?

That is a very deep question. To make a long story short: the idea of Truth is very abstract. We can relate truth to honesty, conscience, and fairness. But how much honesty, conscience, and fairness do we see in this world? Not much at all. Historically, the one major reality of this material world is unfairness and dishonesty. The human mind has to be quite mature in order to embrace all existing unfairness as a harmonious part of a bigger picture.

The idea of God as a creator of everything is more easily understood than the idea of Truth. Our mind is capable of creating images of God as a Creator, Father, Parent, Spirit, Light, or Absolute. However our imagination fails when attempting to visually conceptualize the idea of Absolute Truth.

So, it is no coincidence that God has a human image in many cultures, as people can easy relate to a human form emotionally and mentally. The sad part of this is that people often confuse this image with God himself. Thus, they limit the idea of Ultimate Truth to the level of their personal understanding. Then they start fighting with others over their overly narrow perception of "truth".

The moment we understand that God, as Truth, has always consisted of far more than our current ideas and experiences, we begin trying to keep our mind open and question everything including our own beliefs.

Can you imagine how different our world could be if all people had a sincere desire to know Truth? If all people could understand that their ideas of God are not yet God, but rather historical interpretations of Truth; how much easier would it be for humankind to live in harmony with each other, naturally embracing the abundance of all existing information about God and Truth?

Instead, we have thousands of religious and spiritual teachings, which compete for the possession of Truth. According to the Center for Study of Global Christianity in 2012, there were 43,000 exclusively Christian denominations, a number that does not even include the thousands of other religions practiced around the world.

Would it be possible to have thousands of truths? Of course not, because Truth must be always singular, and never plural. However, it is still okay to have millions of interpretations of the idea of truth. The crucial point is to know the difference between interpretations and the real Truth.

There is an overwhelming variety of interpretations of the Truth. It can be confusing, although not harmful until human ego causes fights for rightness and domination. On the other hand, such conflicts also serve as mind-boggling evidence that people thirst to understand what is right and what is wrong, what is actually true and what is not.

13.

Two sides of one coin

"You interpret this world through observations, either objective reality or subjective experiences. You may call those interpretations scientific discoveries or divine insights. They all describe Me."
God

We have already discussed that traditional debates on science and religion barely clarify anything; instead they create more confusion and a strong impression that science and religion have been in unbridgeable conflict for ages. No wonder many confused people often ask if there is a chance that science and religion will finally coexist one day. The simple answer is 'yes.' In reality, science and religion have been coexisting since humankind appeared on Earth.

For thousands of years, science and religion have served people without crossing one another. They simply had different roles within human society.

Since the very beginning, science has explored the laws that rule the physical world. Observations of nature, such as discovering its patterns and cycles, were the first pre-scientific methodology that helped people improve such practical skills as hunting and navigation. Later, once people learned to farm and trade crops for meat and fish, they began to develop such sciences as astronomy, agriculture, and mathematics. The first calendars, first measuring systems, first weather forecasts, as well as understanding geographical directions – these were the roots of all future sciences.

If the sciences have supplemented daily human life in a practical manner, the role of religion has been very different. First of all, spiritual and religious beliefs, at their root, serve mainly to meet humanity's need to understand reality as a holistic system.

Do you know that understanding is the most important function of human beings? Our every action or re-action is a result of our understanding of how things should be. Our primitive ancestors needed to understand how to survive within their hostile environment. They also needed to know how to communicate with each other, because it was much easier to survive together instead of alone.

The first people expressed their intuitive insights and dreams of abundant prey through primitive cave drawings. Their belief in a higher power, one that provided people with life and food, was the cradle of future religions.

Religions helped people make sense of their lives. We cannot even imagine how hard it was to live thousands years ago when grueling labor, hunger, and epidemics were considered normal. Religions gave people meaning, ideology, and a structure for their lives. They defined social hierarchies and moral standards.

Western history knows only a couple episodes when science and religion, as two systems of knowledge, actually clashed. One such controversy was Galileo's trial on the heliocentric model of universe; another was due to Darwin's theory of evolution.

Historically, both of these conflicts were natural. For thousands of years, science was at the stage of its early development and had no sufficient proof to explain the planetary life.

So, religion explained everything. And we have to admit that the old religious myths were formed logically. They logically reflected what ordinary people could observe: a blue dome sky on top of a flat Earth, around which everything revolves: stars, the moon, the Milky Way, and the magnificent Sun. This interpretation was supported by ancient scripts, so it became a dogmatic postulate to explain how things ought to be.

Eventually, science came up with a new heliocentric model. It stated that the sun, rather than the Earth, was in the middle of our universe. Most importantly, the heliocentric theory was proven by formulas. It was the first serious intellectual challenge for the never-before-criticized religious dogmas.

In 1543, Nicklaus Copernicus' treatise "On the Revolutions of the Heavenly Spheres" began what we now call the scientific revolution; it was at this point that science became more than a supplement for human existence. At this time, the idea of Truth was separated from religion and started its own life. The search for Truth through exploring the physical world became the goal of developing sciences.

Three hundred years later, Darwin's work on the theory of evolution and the origin of species presented the second serious challenge for religious dogmas; now science competed with the religious idea of creation, not only of the world, but people as well.

The scientific position looked far more legitimate here. It was supported by archaeological and other data. In turn, religions could not offer more than the different myths, including the story of Adam and Eve.

In the course of time and with the further development of scientific disciplines, religion and science had to redefine their spheres of influence.

In the 20th century, science became the ultimate authority on Truth in regards to the physical world.

Religion's dominion in western countries has narrowed to an intangible realm of our thoughts and feelings as well as ideas about the meaning of life, salvation, the after-life, and morality.

At the same time, science as a system of unbiased knowledge has no means to objectively analyze personal mystical experiences, so science cannot prove or disprove the majority of religious interpretations. As a system of objective knowledge, science is silent.

Today, science and religion have no reasons for new arguments. They supplement each other and continue their peaceful co-existence.

14.

Why do people leave their religions?

> *"I'm not your religion. When you leave your denomination, don't reject Me."*
> ***God***

An interesting conundrum: if there is no real competition between science and religion, then why are millions of people leaving their denominations? Why are arguments about God, Truth, science, and religion more intense than ever before?

It is important to uncover the real conflict that generates all these arguments and causes people to abandon their churches.

According to the 2012 Pew Research Center poll, the number of Americans who leave their traditional religions grows at a rapid pace. 33 million people (about 14% of adults) described their religious beliefs as "nothing in particular."13 millions described themselves as atheists and agnostics. That is nearly 6% of the U.S. public..

The question is: why this is such a strong trend? Why are many churches losing their congregations and being forced to close?

It would not be exaggeration to say that the religious system in America is probably the best in the world: it is diverse, politically correct, not oppressive, tolerant to alternative beliefs, and very active and helpful in local communities. Isn't that beautiful? It's not one of those oppressive autocratic religious regimes that have existed in some countries, one in which people have to protest and fight for their religious freedom.

The good news is that there is nothing much to protest in America. People already have their freedom of speech and freedom of religion. If you do not like one denomination, just cross the street and try another one. It is like a grand religious buffet with thousands of religious traditions, sprinkled with ceremonies, singing, meditations, and prayers!

What makes people leave their religious organizations and start rambling around to search for something that would satisfy their mind and make their heart happy?

The biggest problem is the problem of understanding. Modern people have far too many questions when compared to their ancestors. Our ancestors were comfortable simply obeying the authority of their church. They had no scientific explanations for lightning, the changing of seasons, or other natural phenomena. They knew that an understanding of God was impossible as well. They were handed the truth to believe, and did not ask for more.

Today we live in an informational, democratic society where nothing is safe from questioning. Such mentality is formed by education based on scientific ideas and the absolute authority of science. We know that scientific postulates are truthful because they are logically proven.

The idea that Truth had to be logically proven is deeply embedded in our subconscious mind. When we read religious books, our mind automatically tries to combine logically ancient stories with all of the informational baggage we have accumulated over many years.

If earlier religions were separated from each other due to their geographical locations, today all of them are in one place called Internet. It is possible to compare their history, traditions, and ideas on Truth or God, all while comfortably sitting at home.

Inevitably such religious diversity is very confusing. It makes us question where the actual Truth is and how to know it when we find it.

The situation becomes even more challenging for the mind to comprehend when some religious doctrines insist that the literal perception of ancient stories is the only possible way to Truth.

For instance, the story of sacrificing God's own child to save millions of sinners was, until recently, perceived as evidence of the highest love.

Today this dogmatic statement is one of the favorite targets for atheistic mockery: how kind could God be if He is capable of killing His own child to save others from His own anger? Well, such a literal interpretation definitely makes no sense. And that is just only one example out of many.

There is an expression used in sales: a confused mind doesn't buy. The same is true for religion; many people leave religions because of their confusion. They cannot just believe one "truth" today in a Buddhist temple, another "truth" tomorrow in a Muslim mosque, and a third "truth" next week in a Catholic cathedral.

Our mind is not able to logically unite all of these religious interpretations of truths and scientific knowledge into one concept. We need logical explanations and proofs to understand what is really true.

As only science offers a logical understanding of physical reality, many people feel that they should make their choice in favor of science, as Sunday sermons failed to make God available to them.

Thus, a lack of understanding is the main problem that underlies this exodus of modern people from their religions. Modern, science-based perception struggles to rationally embrace ancient interpretations of God.

As a result, many either seek out their own truth through alternative spiritual teachings or they fall into a classic atheistic trap: along with their religion, they also threw away the very idea of God. They misunderstand that God is not a religious image or a story, but rather the initial law and cause of all creation.

15.

Why do you need God?

> _"I wish I could give people love, money, health and whatever they are praying for right that moment, but... I'm not a vending machine."_
> _God_

There is also another problem related to understanding, albeit indirectly.

We once took the opportunity to talk with a group of students about their personal disappointments with their religions. Several people shared their realization that going to church and praying was a waste of time. If they prayed to ask for something and never received results, then why would they need God?

Honestly, for me at that moment, such a childish approach to God and religion was a sheer revelation. What else could be expected from kids who were raised in our secular society, which is all about consumption and instant gratification? Do you want to warm your home? You do not need to chop wood in order to kindle fire in your fireplace. Simply turn on a heater. Do you want pizza? Call the pizza place!

Do you want to chat with your friend? Dial her number. Do you want to know the latest news or weather forecast?

Just get your smart phone out of your pocket... These instantaneous technological miracles have become second nature for everyone, so those who have never been introduced to the idea of God may often suggest that God, as the most powerful being, cannot possibly lag behind a pizza delivery and has to provide miracles at a speed that competes with modern technology.

If students have never attended church with their parents, and have never heard much about God and religions at school, how would they know that God is not a vending machine that distributes your every wish in return for the currency of prayer?

This naïve pragmatism is not far from the cavemen's relationships with their wooden gods, who before hunting might say: "Dear gods, I'm giving you sacrificial offerings – be sure to provide a good prey, otherwise I will beat you when I'm back."

For many, the concept that our consumption is not everything in this life and that God is not related to such things is enormous and hard to digest. It can be called spiritual infantilism, and is another reason why some people leave churches, disappointed with a God who was promising love, but was unwilling to provide their daily bread or at least a bit of luck.

The third reason why people leave their congregations is actually not religious. It is no secret that some people need their church only as a place for habitual social gatherings. As soon as people meet some social conflict or disagreement with other members of their congregation, nothing remains to keep them there. They leave their congregation as others might leave a country club, and start looking for a nicer community where they can continue having a good time on weekends.

16.

History vs. 'New' American atheists

> *"There is no such thing as the lack of logic.*
> *There is a lack of personal understanding."*
> *God*

As a result of this exodus, the number of those who abandon God along with their denomination has grown rapidly. Among this new generation of young American adults, it has become popular to label yourself as an "atheist" or even a "new American atheist."

As Americans don't have a history of atheism, they usually lack the deep historical understanding of what atheism can become when it is projected from the personal rejection of God into social reality. Due to this shallow understanding of atheism, the word "atheist" has an attractive aura of independent thinking, freedom from religious authority, and even freedom from old-fashioned moral norms for many modern opponents of religion.

When American atheists passionately attack religious scripts, dogmas, or traditions, they usually present themselves as proponents of science. Many of them connect their lack of *personal* belief in God with the lack of *scientific evidence* of God's existence, much in the same way that Russian atheists did a century ago. Regardless of their culture or time period, atheists miss the point that these issues are neither related to each other nor to the existence of God.

As a Russian who was born in the Soviet Union, the largest communist empire, where atheism was the official ideology, I would like to share with you a bit of Russian history and how it happened that the entire Russian Orthodox Empire one day turned upside down and transformed into an atheistic nerve center.

I believe the devastating tragedy of the Russian nation that had to survive decades of communism is an important historical example of how scientific ideas were used to camouflage a horrible atheistic regime and justify its cruel ideology. In reality, Russian atheism had nothing to do with science and its mission to discover the truth about the world.

Until the revolution (1917), the Russian Orthodox Church was a significant part of the Russian autocratic political system. It required all Russians, not only believers, to implicitly obey religious rules and dogmas. It was a very rigid and corrupt system that did not best exemplify the Christian values of love, truth, and tolerance.

A century ago, the Russian church was known for its extreme hostility toward progressive thought. On one hand, this centralized religion was responsible for the state education system. At the same time, it would not even recognize the new heliocentric theory and it certainly would not consider alternative views on creation.

You can understand how annoying it was for educated people to have this religious monster in their faces.

By the 20th century, Darwin's ideas were in the forefront of progressive thought and occupied the minds of millions. Along with the heliocentric system, the Darwinian theories on evolution and origins of species directly contradicted the literal perception of the Bible's stories about the creation of the world in six days and about the creation of mankind; namely, the story of Adam and Eve.

As previously stated, science had no other theories that would challenge religious scripts, dogmas, or beliefs. However, heliocentric theory and the theory of evolution were enough to trigger overwhelming protest, though not against religious (in this case, Christian) beliefs, but mostly against the pressure and politics of the reactive religious system.

If the Russian church was not afraid to lose its political power, the conflict might have ended with a discussion about the literal perception of old stories and new scientific data. Alas, this was not the case. The religious authorities were not willing to compromise either their political power or traditional religious interpretations even a bit.

Now, imagine crowds of angry people whose ideas of science or religion were very shallow, and based mostly on comics and grotesque disputes from cheap yellow newspapers.

All they knew was that science had proved that Earth was round and that it revolved around Sun. They had also heard there was a scientific discussion about people evolving from apes. They did not care if Darwin's theory was proven or not. The mind-blowing information about "ape-ancestors" was everything they needed to fight their hated political system. Therefore it was not a big deal to jump to the overall conclusion that science disproved God's existence and religion was wrong.

There is no one to blame. Human minds are programmed to logically justify whatever people want.

This was how primitive atheism started: A bit of science, a lot of confusion, and plenty of disagreement regarding religious rules, dogmas and illogical claims about Truth.

The problem grew out of the fact that the crowd mentality was unable to distinguish the idea of "God" from the idea of "Religion." When people emotionally fight for their ideas, they are unable to see that "God" as universal Law differs from the idea of "Religion" as a manmade institution.

The Russians threw out the proverbial baby with the bath water: they destroyed religion and, along with that, they rejected God.

We all know about the results: the overall atheism and oppressive communist regime reigned to nearly to the end of the 20th century, leaving in its wake millions of victims and a destroyed culture.

Let's highlight something important out of this short historical digression: the conflict between science and religion did not cause the Russian revolution. Instead, the revolution began with a newly born, science-based mentality that confronted an oppressive and corrupt religious system. This conflict was exacerbated by the media, who added fire to the Russian civil war. Later, the false idea of conflict between science and religion had become the cornerstone of atheistic dogmas and politics.

It is easy to manipulate the masses, because crowd mentality is incredibly superficial. People do not think much. They would rather trust authorities, who know how to bend logic and play the crowd's emotions. Communists put science on the banner of atheist propaganda to look progressive and rebel not only against the religious views, but also everyone who disagreed with the communist regime.

The bold and deceitful statement, "science has proven there is no God" was unquestionable communist dogma that was reinforced through education from the first day of kindergarten through graduation from university.

I find it very interesting that religious or atheistic fundamentalists can argue passionately for or against God's existence, but they usually do not really care about the Truth.

After seven long decades of atheistic brain washing, the communist empire of the Soviet Union finally collapsed.

This time, no one fought against religion or atheism; I think the Russians were fed up with every ideology. I have never heard Russians debating religion, science, or atheism. Additionally, I do not know any Russians who would be proud of their atheistic views and excited to fight against God. Can new atheists bring any new perspective or ideas that had not been used by Soviet communists in the last century? I doubt it. Lately, I personally have not heard anything new on atheism in either America or Russia. I hope Russia got its atheism vaccination and that people are now ready to look for Truth.

17.

Have you ever seen a monster under a bed?

"If you want to <u>understand</u> Me, be honest and logical in your search for Truth. If you want to <u>know</u> Me – just talk to Me personally from your deepest sincerity."
God

If science and religion peacefully coexist and people can leave their denominations searching for a "more understandable Truth," then the question is still there: what fuels these debates and creates the impression that science and religion never stop fighting?

I would like to make a point here. Until people claim their exclusivity on Truth, there is no conflict.

Have you ever heard about passionate debates between science and Buddhism or Hinduism? I haven't. Buddhism and Hinduism gently offer the ways to truth and wisdom without claiming any exclusivity of their views over science or other religions. Maybe that is the reason why those spiritual teachings are becoming more and more popular in the West.

Science does not lay any exclusive claim on Truth either. Instead, science is dedicated to discovering the Truth through unbiased and objective methods. In the scientific world, all theories are perceived as *current* interpretations of reality. They can be reconsidered if new, contradictory data comes to light.

Looking closely at the debates and religion-related conflicts, we will easily see that most arguments have been between atheism and the three Abrahamic religions: Judaism, Christianity, and Islam.

All four claim exclusive knowledge of the Truth and fight others who disagree, including each other.

Why do not believers or even fundamentalists fight against science in the 21st century?

The answer is simple: to do so would be insane. Firstly, science does not step on the toes of any deity. Secondly, nobody fights science because we all have scientifically-based perceptions regardless of how we identify ourselves: believers, non-believers, agnostics, atheists, seekers...

It is a very interesting perceptional phenomenon. People with the same scientifically-based perceptions and similar education can take opposing stances regarding the existence of God.

Why does it happen?

System Outlook states we cannot understand God until we understand the principles of our perception and the role of our personal experiences and interpretations.

There is a conventional opinion that human beliefs and feelings are irrational. Often it seems our beliefs, feelings, and emotions come out of nowhere. They possess our mind and body, making us to say and do irrelevant things that later we might regret. Why does it happen that at the moment we believe something, we start fighting for our vision of Truth and become blind to any alternative information or even common sense?

It is possible to rationally explain how our mind generates beliefs when we understand how the system of perception works.

The concept of System Outlook finally cracks this mystery by offering such understanding.

If you saw Santa Claus when you were three years old, and that Christmas Santa gave you a big toy truck or a Barbie princess with long golden hair, you would probably believe in Santa like all kids do, as they do not yet know the details about where "Santa" gets all the toys.

This same logic applies to other beliefs as well. If you personally saw an angel, extraterrestrial, or monster under your bed, it would become an absolute truth for you, because you personally experienced this incredible event. Others can have any opinions on that. They can say that your experience was impossible, that you were drunk, stoned, crazy, or dreaming.

For our personal memory, others' opinions are irrelevant. Impressions from life experiences stay in our memory forever, although, in time, human memory can play a lot of tricks with our past impressions, combining them or wiping them out entirely.

However, if you had a really strong experience related to a materialistic world or to the "spiritual" world, no one will ever be able to convince you that it was just your imagination.

That is what happens to those who become true believers. They experience something profound and personal. It is called a 'spiritual' or 'mystical' experience.

They might not be able to explain it, but that does not matter. All that matters is the fact that something special really happened to them, changed their life, and it was not imaginary at all.

18.

Did you have "THAT" experience or not yet?

"Your ability to give up your rightness and surrender to Me, is the gate you allow Me in."
God

Let me share a short story about my close friend and her husband. Years ago, my friends were young, materialistic, and not at all religious or spiritual. They were typical products of the Soviet atheist mentality. If someone would tell them about God or a spiritual journey, they would be annoyed rather than interested. I would not call them strong atheists, as they did not care to argue about religion or God. They simply did not care about these subjects at all. So, I did not talk to them about spirituality. I knew their faces would express nothing but cynical grins and boredom.

They were around twenty-six years old when they found themselves in the midst of huge turmoil. They suddenly lost their business and barely had enough money for the bus. In 1990, during Perestroika, Russia was flooded with crime. My friends, like the majority of other people, could not avoid it.

The mafia threatened them, and they were forced to hide.

After six months of hiding from the mafia, their despair reached its breaking point. They had no choice but to kneel in the middle of their apartment and, for the first time in either of their lives, pray to God. God had become their last hope. That was also the first time when both of them had a chain of spiritual experiences that totally changed their system of beliefs, and inevitably their lives.

As an "objective" result, the mafia suddenly left them alone for no apparent reason. My friends got a chance to start a new life and its quality was changed at its very core. They both became very strong believers to the point that, years later, my friend's husband was seriously thinking about becoming a minister. For more than a decade they have woken up early on Sundays in order to attend sermons at their church, more than an hour away.

You have probably heard similar stories from some of your friends as well. Let's be logical: there is no theoretical knowledge, Bible school, or preacher that could convince people to change their life so dramatically, especially if those people are atheists who previously did not care about God at all!

Talking *about* God is very different from feeling the divine presence. You can learn all of the theological and philosophical ideas possible; however, without at least some personal experience of divine presence, your faith is not yet alive. It is more scholarly and impersonal compared to faith of those who develop intimate personal relationship with this highest universal power.

The point of this story is simple. The only difference between an atheist and a true believer is a profound ***personal mystical (or spiritual) experience***, nothing more or less. After your personal memory records such an experience, which cannot be disregarded by your mind, there is no way back to rejecting or doubting God.

It is naïve to think that hundreds of millions of people, who truly believe in their version of God, just pretend to have faith or lie when they speak of their relationship with the spiritual realm. There is no sense for doing it! There is no sense in praying to an "imaginary" God or following any of His commandments or religious rules if you do not feel there is something real on that side.

The amount of existing religions and spiritual teachings is the best evidence that phenomena of personal spiritual experiences exist, and that those who are open to these experiences find them in one form or another, regardless of their cultural or religious traditions, language, education, or era.

The problem is that those experiences and their interpretations are subjective, as a single person is the only observer who can feel and register this experience. However, the *effect* of such experiences is objective because others can observe it too.

19.
A 'logical' leap to wrong conclusion

"When you feel My presence, just simply witness that you personally know Me. Do not assume that your religion is My only dwelling. There is no bottle that can house an elephant."
God

What is the difference between true believers and fundamentalists of all types if faith in God is based on personal experiences for both of these groups?

I would say that a "healthy" belief in God comes from honest observation and establishing your personal relationship with God. It is accompanied by sincere respect toward other people's experiences, as well as understanding that God, as a single initial source of everything for all alive creatures, has endless ways of communication with His creations.

In contrary, fundamentalists are those who cannot embrace, even theoretically, that there are different experiences of divine presence with the same value and importance as their own. Fundamentalism as a rejection of all alternative beliefs is a religious form of fanaticism.

How do people become fundamentalists? When one has a strong spiritual experience within a specific religious group or within a temple, his mind jumps to the *wrong* conclusion: that his spiritual experience was a divine proof of truthfulness of that specific religion and its theological doctrine.

From this perspective, atheism is no different. It is a materialistic opposition to fundamentalism. Atheism is based on the belief there is no God. This belief is formed not by science as atheists proclaim; *atheistic belief is based on the lack of the same personal spiritual experiences and the lack of current scientific evidence.*

20.

One destructive mind-trickster

"You are more than your mind. You are more than what you think. Observe how the computer of your mind creates your opinions and your self-identity."
God

Our beliefs about this world, right and wrong, and how things should be, depend on all of our past experiences and impressions. If someone's childhood was immersed in an atmosphere of a wise, loving, and caring family, that person's expectations of life are usually much more positive compared to the worldview of those who were abandoned as children and who knew only hunger, abuse, and violence.

One of the subconscious functions of human perception that creates our beliefs is generalization. It is important to be aware of how generalization works. Generalization creates personal projections regarding surrounding reality and our future, making one simple logical suggestion: if something happened once in my life and it is true for me, it has to be objective reality and true for everyone.

Such subjective or inductive reasoning is the essence of generalization and it is based solely on what we know personally. On one hand, generalization is very important and we could not survive another day without this function. When we learn how drive a car, we make a logical suggestion that all the other cars have to be driven the same way due to generalization. Or, before going to bed, we know we will wake up tomorrow because, due to generalization, our mind makes a subconscious assumption: if we have already woken up thousands of times before, the next morning we will wake up again.

Generalization creates our vision of the world and beliefs about reality. If we look at our perception from this vantage point, we will see that our beliefs are nothing but logical patterns that were reinforced by our memory multiple times, either through actual experiences or mental imaginary repetition, or both. For instance, when our mind repeats many times the same scene of a horrible crime from the recent news, we start believing that life must be a pure nightmare. This is the manner in which people create their personal ideas of truth.

When people deal with the materialistic reality of human society or nature, generalization usually works perfectly because materialistic reality is based on natural and manmade laws. It is understandable because laws and patterns create predictable results.

However, our *subconscious* mind does not know the difference between deductive and inductive reasoning, or between real and imaginary events. It is the reason why generalization can become a destructive mind-trickster, which generates negative beliefs that are related not to objective reality, but only to our personal past experiences, emotions, and imagination.

For instance, if someone has had several failed relationships due to their partners' dishonesty and betrayal, and memory holds those experiences coupled with plenty of negative emotions, subconscious generalization can jump to the overall unquestionable belief that *all* men (or women) are "liars" unworthy of trust. People often feel like these opinions are absolute Truth, and they do not require any other objective logical proofs from the outside.

Generalization of personal experiences is the root cause of our feeling of rightness and the sincere belief we know better than others what is true.

Closed-mindedness, stubbornness, fanaticism, and negativism are based on personal generalizations that go unquestioned. To notice how our personal experiences become "absolute truth," we need to make ***conscious effort and use unbiased logic***. Only then we can see that a conclusion from failed relationships would logically sound more like, "I haven't *yet* experienced the real love" and not "there *is no* real love in the world."

The same pattern is applicable to the lack of mystical or spiritual experiences. The correct logical conclusion would be *"I haven't yet experienced the real connection with God"* instead of the wrong generalization *there is no God.*

Many people miss the very important point that *a lack of knowledge about a subject means only the lack of knowledge or evidence, not the lack of the subject itself.* In contrast with many debaters, true scientists are very accurate with their statements. They do not say unicorns cannot exist. They say only that today's science does not have proof of, and cannot say anything about unicorns. Who knows, maybe a hundred years later people will find genetically replicated unicorns in a zoo that would look exactly like their prototypes from movies about Harry Potter! Human history has enough examples which show that what is impossible or improvable today can be a reality tomorrow. Flights to the Moon are the perfect example of this.

21.

What if…

"Always practice honesty. It is a shortcut to amazing insights and discoveries."
God

I remember I was in elementary school when I asked my mother if there was a God. She became silent for a moment and then told me how her grandmother had taught her to pray to God when no one was watching them in early 1950.

However, praying to God as a small girl did not bring my mother any mystical experiences that would convince her God is real. So, her answer was honest and simple: "I don't know if there is a God."

It was the first time I saw my parents not supporting the official ideology and common beliefs that were drummed into our heads at school. Her honesty left the door to God open: what if God really exists? What if all teachers at school are wrong? What if my illiterate great grandma was right?.. What if…?

It would be wrong to suggest that the people who insist there is no God are dishonest. My schoolteachers or other atheists might be great, kind, and honest people by nature.

Their problem is misunderstanding that *the lack of personal experiences is not the objective Truth.*

It is a profound thing to realize that our understanding of anything is not Truth, but simply interpretations that reflect the previous experiences we have accumulated in our memory over the years.

I would like to ask you to contemplate the difference between two statements: "Science does not have proof there is a God" and "Science has proven there is no God." These statements sound very similar, though, in reality, the first statement is true and the second one is false.

I remember how the deceitful statement that "science has proven there is no God" was unquestionable communist dogma constantly reinforced through Soviet education and mass media.

People often argue that atheism is a negative religion. I am absolutely convinced atheism is a form of religion because it is based on personal beliefs instead of pure logic. When atheism became the official Soviet ideology, communists made it sacred and justified it with communist "sacred texts." Vladimir Lenin, the leader of Russian revolution, wrote volumes of political articles. Later these articles become a foundation for "scientific communism," which could be called a "communist theology" based on Lenin's quotations.

There are no better words than "science" or "scientifically proven" to add credibility to any product or political idea.

Here is my warning: when you hear the words "science," "scientific," "scientifically proven formula," or any kind of sophisticated terminology - do not be gullible. Simply check what is behind those words, what people are selling you, and how it relates to common sense and solid logic.

Afterward

Coexistence between science and religion is a very complex and emotional subject for many people because it involves questioning the essence of Truth. This book is the beginning of a *productive* conversation about Truth. To wrap up this discussion, I would like to highlight a few points.

1. According to System Outlook, in our universe everything is either a system or a part of a system. Human beings and their perceptions are systems too. To *productively* discuss ultimate questions like Truth, God, or the meaning of life, we need to use an ultimate neutral scientifically based platform like System Outlook, which principles are applicable to all possible systems.

2. When we have controversial issues that involve a lot of discussion and emotion, it is crucial to *clearly define what we are actually debating*. In order to do this the proper way, we should separate a complex problem into segments, which are different systems that are related to the discussed issue. It is important to honestly question our impressions and opinions within the system approach in order to discover the root of the conflict.

In the case of science and religion, the system approach helps us understand there is no conflict. With the exception of a few theoretical clashes, these two different knowledge systems have coexisted peacefully and supplemented each other for thousands of years.

3. Due to the system approach, we can clearly see that religions as political systems differ from religions as beliefs systems. There is no need to blame God, prophets, or religious teachings for crimes committed by religious organizations. For instance, the Spanish Inquisition was a result of a political religious system and was not related to Christ or the system of Christian beliefs.

4. Be very attentive when people use the word "science." *Science is not related to atheism* and atheism is not a new American phenomenon. Instead, it was an official communist ideology that was deeply experienced by billions of people in 20th century Russia, Eastern Europe, China, etc.

5. Most people only become true believers after having personal mystical experiences. Personal mystical experiences (or lack thereof) cannot be considered *objective* proof of God's existence or absence. That is the reason why debates between believers and atheists are never productive, as they are based on witnessing the

opposite parties' personal experiences. So, until believers or atheists claim their exclusive right on truth, there is no conflict.

6. According to System Outlook, *science and religion both interpret the eternal laws of universal Truth either through objective scientific observations or subjective personal experiences.* Though there is no real conflict between science and religion as two knowledge systems, there are still *perceptional problems* that cause the illusion of confrontation.

The lack of religious reconciliation is the root reason, which causes the illusion that science and religion are in conflict. This happens because modern, scientifically-based perceptions cannot logically embrace multiple religious interpretations of truth.

7. System Outlook can be a conceptual platform for religious reconciliation because it views science and all existing religions as neutral informational systems, which are formed by the same principles of human perception.

***

Thank you for reading this book.

I deeply respect those who think. Let's stay in touch.

If you would like to share your thoughts or be the first to get new materials or books of System Outlook series for *free* at the time they are released on Amazon-Kindle, please join our group on Facebook.com, which has the same name: "Science and religion can coexist" or sign up on our websites www.ScienceAndReligonCoexist.com or www.SystemOutlook.com

If you enjoy contemplation, I also invite you to learn more about this revolutionary system-informational theory of everything from the initial book "System Outlook. The New Original World View Based on a System-Informational Approach. Description of a concept" by Elena Iam.

The book is available on Amazon.com in English and Russian languages as a paperback or Kindle edition.

Thank you.

The Ultimate Model of System-Informational Matrix

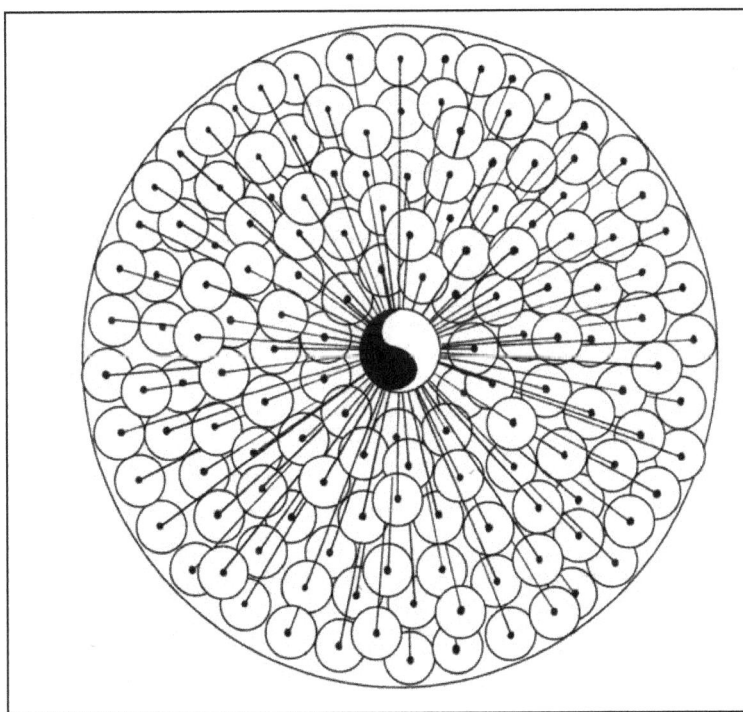

For notes & questions without answers

"In dual reality, every question has an answer. Some answers simply need time before they are revealed and embraced by human mind."

God

_____

_____

_____

_____

_____

_____

_____

_____

_____

_____

_____

_____

_____

_____

_____

Invite Elena to speak at your event!

Elena Iam is an author, educator, and speaker on the most controversial topics that have sparked debates for thousands of years.

Elena's presentations are genuine, thought-provoking and interactive. They are filled with new insights and ideas guaranteed to captivate and inspire your audience. Her talks are ideal for conferences, workshops, seminars, lectures series, campus clubs, summer programs, and any kind of discussions.

Elena introduces a new system-informational perspective on traditional debates, atheism and the nature of beliefs. She involves people in the dialogue regarding the deepest questions of life: what we are, what is truth, why do we have to suffer, and so on...

Elena helps others face controversial ideas with an open mind and without resentment toward other opinions. There are no 'difficult' or unwelcomed questions to discuss.

Elena would be happy to tailor the message of her presentation to a specific theme of your event. Her talks can range from one-hour to two-day workshop, whatever fits your schedule.

To contact Elena regarding speaking engagements or books orders, please send her a request through her website

www.**ScienceAndReligionCoexist**.com

or connect to her through www.FaceBook.com

www.Facebook.com/SystemOutlook

Elena's Most Requested Presentations

Yes! Science and religion can coexist!

It's the most popular, largely requested topic. What is the real conflict that fuels so many debates regarding God and science? What makes people leave their denominations? What do atheism and fundamentalism have in common? Is there a way to religious reconciliation?

Can science prove the existence of God?

Why do traditional natural and physical sciences fail to prove God? And, is it possible for system sciences to bridge the gap?

Science, faith, and atheism. Where does atheism come from?

Why do people leave religioin and become atheists? Is atheism related to science?

Science and the mystery of the meaning of life

Is the meaning of life objective? How does the meaning of life differ from other important values? What do science and religion say about it?

Free will and the Initial Law – religious and scientific perspectives

Ethical laws: what do they have in common with gravity? How do systems define freedom?

The philosophy of Elena's talks is revolutionary, though very simple. It's based on two new axioms that everything in our universe is either a system or a part of a system and we are informational beings, whose main function is understanding.